Pocket Books

Mammals

Kane Miller
A DIVISION OF EDC PUBLISHING

First American Edition 2015
Kane Miller, A Division of EDC Publishing

Copyright © Green Android Ltd 2014

For information contact:
Kane Miller, A Division of EDC Publishing
P.O. Box 470663
Tulsa, OK 74147-0663
www.kanemiller.com
www.edcpub.com
www.usbornebooksandmore.com

All rights reserved. No part of this publication may be reproduced, stored in a retrieval system, or transmitted in any form or by any means, electronic, mechanical, photocopying, recording or otherwise without the prior written permission of the publisher.

Please note that every effort has been made to check the accuracy of the information contained in this book, and to credit the copyright holders correctly. Green Android Ltd apologize for any unintentional errors or omissions, and would be happy to include revisions to content and/or acknowledgements in subsequent editions of this book.

Printed and bound in China, December 2018
6 7 8 9 10 11 12 13 14 15
Library of Congress Control Number: 2014939760
ISBN: 978-1-61067-349-5

Images © Fotolia.com: indian rhinoceros © Alan Jeffery; maned wolf, striped hyena © anankkml; yak © andreyshot; bottlenose dolphin © avs_lt; alpine marmot © barbarawelsch; short-eared elephant shrew © belizar; arctic wolf © bmaynard; olive baboon © bobschalkwijk; wild boar, moose © byrdyak; collared peccary © Christian Musat; reindeer © Clément Billet; african wild dog © Debbie Aird Photography; blue wildebeest © dennisjacobsen; greater kudu © dr322; black rhinoceros © EcoPrint; black flying fox © EcoView; european rabbit © Eduardo Rivero; polar bear © erectus; emperor tamarin © Eric Gevaert; aardvark © Eric Isselée; eastern cottontail © Fexel; black wildebeest © forcdan; rocky mountain goat © Fun Altitude; leopard seal © Gentoo Multimedia; roan antelope © Gerrit de Vries; american black bear © gsamurai2931; fennec fox © Hagit Berkovich; lowland streaked tenrec, nine-banded armadillo, indri © hakoar; meerkat © Henry Brown; eurasian red squirrel © hfox; capybara © ijdema; leopard © ingridd313; markhor © JackF; south american tapir © Jan Gottwald; burchell's zebra © Jean-Marc Strydom; proboscis monkey © Kjersti; tiger © kyslynskyy; giant panda © leungchopan; bighorn sheep © Marina Krasnovid; black spider monkey © michaklootwijk; minke whale © mojo_jojo; european mole © mradlgruber; african buffalo © Natalia Pushchina; brown bear © Onkelchen; arctic fox © outdoorsman; common warthog © Pal Teravagimov; greater slow loris © pattarasiri virayasi; giant pangolin © petert2; brown-throated sloth © photographee2000; red fox, fallow deer © Pim Leijen; verreaux's sifaka © Rich Lindie; common chimpanzee © Ronnie Howard; guanaco © RyszardStelmachowicz; clouded leopard © Sarah Cheriton-Jones; stoat © Stephan Morris; cheetah © Stu Porter; european hedgehog © suerob; spotted hyena © tiero; bornean orangutan © Uryadnikov Sergey; eurasian beaver © vchphoto; red deer © veneratio; asiatic black bear © Vibe Images; american pika, puma © visceralimage; raccoon dog © XK.

Images © shutterstock.com: northern river otter © Ginger Livingston Sanders; alpine ibex © Robert Asento; ocelot © Andy Poole; przewalski's wild horse © Anita Huszti; sea otter © bierchen; eurasian water shrew © CreatureNature.nl; red howler monkey © David Davis; dingo © Eleanor; golden lion tamarin © Eric Gevaert; wolverine © Erik Mandre; striped skunk © Heiko Kiera; bobcat © Holly Kuchera; ring-tailed lemur © Hugh Lansdown; red panda © Hung Chung Chih; african bush elephant © Johan Swanepoel; malayan tapir © Lionack Bruno; honey badger © Meoita; coyote © BGSmith; western lowland gorilla © Mike Price; asiatic elephant © Mogens Trolle; grévy's zebra © Nick Biemans; bactrian camel, dromedary camel © Nurlan Kalchinov; rock hyrax © Peter Wollinga; iberian lynx © Rafa Irusta; red kangaroo © Rafael Ramirez Lee; fishing cat © Sarah Cheriton-Jones; african forest elephant © Sergey Uryadnikov; caracal © Stu Porter; eastern grey squirrel © Stubblefield Photography; euroasian badger © Sue Robinson; northern raccoon © Tom Reichner; dugong © Kristina Vackova; orca © Monika Wieland gaur © Teerapun; american bison © Brian Lasenby; bongo © hallam creations, Bryan Busovicki; giraffe © Bryan Busovicki, hippopotamus © MartinMaritz, lion © LeonP; grey; seal © Clinton Moffat; californian sea lion © Shane W Thompson; walrus © outdoorsman; common chimpanzee © stephen; european hare © Bildagentur Zoonar GmbH; common wombat © David Lade; koala © robert cicchetti, duck-billed platypus © worldswildlifewonders.

Introducing mammals

There are more than 4,000 different species of mammals living on Earth. They are among the most intelligent of all living creatures. Mammals live in a variety of different environments including the ocean, underground and on land. Some mammals, bats for example, can even fly. Humans are mammals, as are some pets and farm animals such as dogs, cows and horses.

The European mole is a mammal that lives underground.

Orcas come to the water's surface to breathe air.

A female lion nurtures her cubs and keeps them close.

Characteristics of mammals

All mammals are vertebrates. This means they have a backbone or a spine. All mammals breathe air. Even the mammals that live in water must come to the surface every now and then to breathe. Mammals are warm-blooded, meaning they regulate their own body temperature. This allows them to live in almost every climate on Earth. All mammals grow hair or fur at some point during their life. Female mammals produce milk to feed their babies. This allows them to spend time with their young and teach them how to survive on their own.

How to use this book

The pages of this book include concise information and key features on mammals from around the world.

Common name (this is the name mostly used)

Scientific name (this is the name of the animal used by scientists)

Factfile (see opposite page)

Page number

Mammal groups (see pages 6-7)

Color photograph

Conservation status (see opposite page)

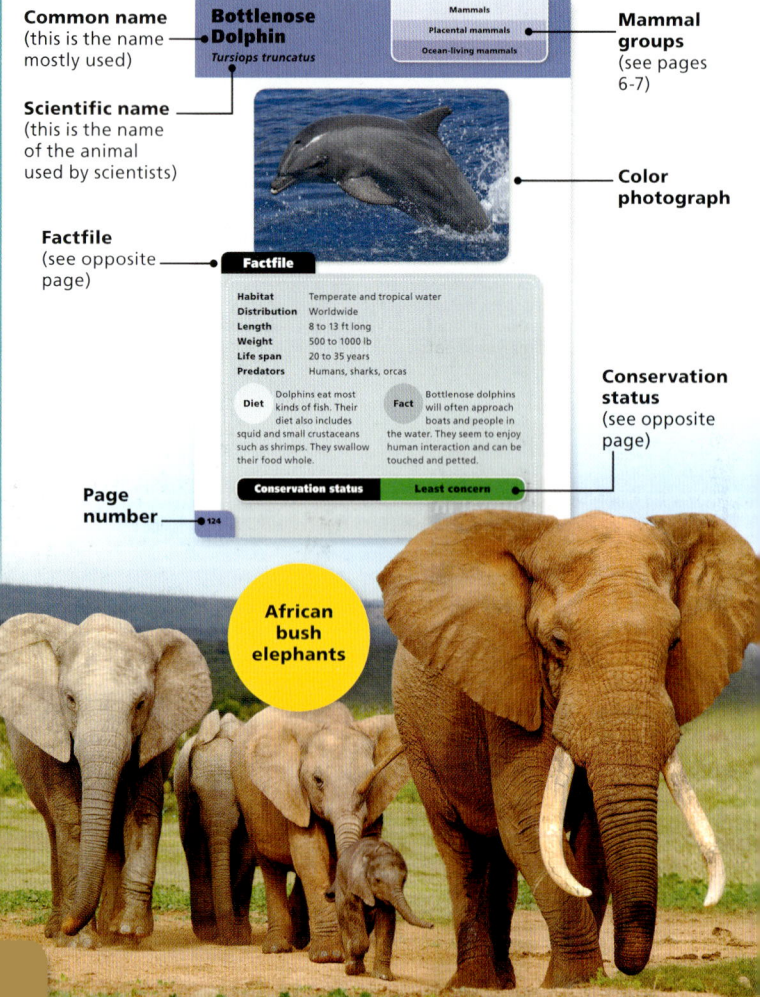

Bottlenose Dolphin
Tursiops truncatus

Mammals
Placental mammals
Ocean-living mammals

Factfile

Habitat	Temperate and tropical water
Distribution	Worldwide
Length	8 to 13 ft long
Weight	500 to 1000 lb
Life span	20 to 35 years
Predators	Humans, sharks, orcas

Diet Dolphins eat most kinds of fish. Their diet also includes squid and small crustaceans such as shrimps. They swallow their food whole.

Fact Bottlenose dolphins will often approach boats and people in the water. They seem to enjoy human interaction and can be touched and petted.

Conservation status — Least concern

124

African bush elephants

Factfile

Each page comes with a detailed factfile containing descriptions, information, facts and figures.

Habitat
This indicates the environment that the mammal lives in.

Distribution
This describes where in the world the mammal lives in its natural habitat.

Size
A measurement of the mammal's body.

Diet
A description of the food that the mammal eats and where it gets the food.

Weight
A measurement of the weight of the mammal.

Life span
This is the average natural length of the mammal's life.

Predators
This category lists the names of other animals that are known to capture and kill this mammal. Some of the smaller mammals often have many predators. When the name of the predator is followed by "(young only)" it indicates that the predator only eats the young of this species.

Fact
Every factfile comes with an interesting fact about each mammal.

Conservation status

Each animal in this book has been given a conservation status. This status indicates the threat of extinction to the species in its native home.

Not evaluated
The animals within this category have not yet been evaluated for their conservation status.

Least concern
This is the lowest risk category. Animals in this category are widespread and abundant.

Near threatened
The animals in this category are likely to become endangered in the near future.

Vulnerable
There is a high risk that animals within this category will become endangered in the wild.

Endangered
There is a high risk that animals within this category will become extinct in the wild.

Critically endangered
There is an extremely high risk of animals in this category becoming extinct in the wild.

Mammal groups

There are three main groups of mammals: monotremes, marsupials and placental mammals. Each group reproduces in different ways.

Monotremes
3 species

This group consists of the duck-billed platypus, the short-beaked echidna and the long-beaked echidna. Monotremes are the only mammals to lay eggs rather than give birth to live young.

Marsupials
272 species

Today, most marsupials are found in Australasia (around 200 species) and Central and South America (around 70 species). Marsupials are commonly thought of as pouched mammals.

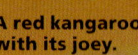

A red kangaroo with its joey.

Placental mammals
Nearly 4,000 species

Placental mammals form the largest and most diverse group of mammals. The mammals within this group have a wide range of body shapes and complex social interactions. The scientific name for placental mammals is eutherians.

A dugong is an example of mammal diversity.

They give birth to live young at an early stage of their development. The newborns crawl up the mother's body and into the safety of the pouch, which is located on her abdomen. Once inside, the baby continues its development for weeks, or even months. Eventually it is large enough to leave the pouch.

Wombats carry their babies in pouches for 5 months.

This large group of mammals includes such diverse animals as whales, elephants, shrews and armadillos. It also includes domestic animals such as cats, dogs, cattle and horses. These mammals give birth to young who are born at an advanced stage. Before birth, the young are nourished through a placenta. The placenta is an organ that delivers oxygen and nutrients to the unborn young.

Contents

Monotremes
Duck-billed platypuses	8

Marsupials
Koalas	9
Wombats	10
Kangaroos	11

Placental mammals
Shrews and their relatives	12
Aardvarks	16
Hyraxes	17
Elephants	18
Armadillos, sloths and pangolins	21
Rabbits, hares and pikas	24
Rodents	28
Primates	33
Bats	46
Hedgehogs	47
Dogs and relatives	48
Bears	57
Sea lions, walruses and seals	62
Raccoons and relatives	66
Cats and relatives	76
Hoofed mammals	89
Ocean-living mammals	122
Sirenians	125

Glossary 126
Index 128

Duck-billed Platypus
Ornithorhynchus anatinus

| Mammals |
| Monotremes |
| Duck-billed platypuses |

Factfile

Habitat   Freshwater creeks, rivers, lakes
Distribution Australia
Size   16 to 24 in long
Weight   1.5 to 5 lb
Life span   15 to 20 years
Predators   Foxes, snakes, crocodiles

Diet The duck-billed platypus eats mostly invertebrates that live on the bottom of lakes, rivers or streams. They will eat some fish and frogs too.

Fact Platypuses are one of only three species of mammal that lay eggs. The others are echidnas, small, spiny land animals that also live in Australia.

Conservation status **Least concern**

- Mammals
- Marsupials
- Koalas

Koala
Phascolarctos cinereus

Factfile

Habitat	Eucalyptus, inland and coastal forest
Distribution	Southeastern Australia
Size	24 to 34 in long
Weight	9 to 33 lb
Life span	15 to 20 years
Predators	Birds of prey, dingoes, humans

Diet The koala has a diet of eucalyptus leaves. These leaves are poisonous to most animals, but koalas have specially adapted digestive systems.

Fact The male has a scent gland on his chest that produces a dark, sticky substance. He rubs this on trees to indicate to others that this is his territory.

Conservation status: Least concern

Common Wombat
Vombatus ursinus

| Mammals |
| Marsupials |
| Wombats |

Factfile

Habitat	Woodland, coastal shrubland
Distribution	Australia
Size	28 to 44 in long
Weight	44 to 77 lb
Life span	20 to 26 years
Predators	Foxes, wild dogs

Diet Wombats feed on grasses, herbs, roots (including roots of grasses, bushes and trees), fungi, shrubs, bark, mosses, leaves and marsh plants.

Fact Wombats are nocturnal, secretive and spend most of their time underground. They live in burrows up to 100 feet long, with several entrances.

Conservation status: Endangered

Mammals
Marsupials
Kangaroos

Red Kangaroo
Macropus rufus

Factfile

Habitat	Scrubland, grassland, desert
Distribution	Australia
Size	3 to 5.5 ft long
Weight	Up to 200 lb
Life span	Up to 22 years
Predators	Humans, dingoes, birds of prey

Diet Red kangaroos are herbivores. They eat grasses, leaves and other vegetation. They mainly feed in the early morning and late afternoon.

Fact Red kangaroos have very powerful legs. They can hop at speeds of 40 miles per hour, leap as far as 26 feet and jump as high as 10 feet!

Conservation status: Least concern

Lowland Streaked Tenrec
Hemicentetes semispinosus

Mammals

Placental mammals

Shrews and their relatives

Factfile

Habitat	Rain forest, scrubland
Distribution	Madagascar
Size	6 to 7.5 in long
Weight	3 to 8 oz
Life span	Up to 2.7 years
Predators	Snakes, mongooses, humans

Diet The lowland streaked tenrec has a diet that is almost exclusively made up of earthworms. Occasionally they will eat other available invertebrates.

Fact They sometimes stamp on the ground with their forepaws. This helps to increase earthworm activity and bring some worms to the surface.

Conservation status — **Least concern**

Mammals
Placental mammals
Shrews and their relatives

Short-eared Elephant Shrew
Macroscelides proboscideus

Factfile

Habitat Desert, semidesert
Distribution Namibia, Botswana, South Africa
Size 4 to 4.5 in long
Weight 1 to 2 oz
Life span 1 to 2 years
Predators Birds of prey

Diet The short-eared elephant shrew is an omnivore. It feeds on insects, berries and plant roots. It mostly forages in the morning and evening.

Fact These shrews have long snouts that resemble an elephant's trunk. Sensitive whiskers around the nostrils help them to locate food.

Conservation status **Least concern**

Eurasian Water Shrew
Neomys fodiens

Mammals

Placental mammals

Shrews and their relatives

Factfile

Habitat	Banks of standing or flowing fresh water
Distribution	Europe, Asia
Size	Up to 4 in long
Weight	Up to .5 oz
Life span	Up to 3 years
Predators	Weasels, cats, owls, foxes

Diet The Eurasian water shrew eats a diet of aquatic insects, small fish and frogs. They will also hunt on land for beetles, earthworms and grubs.

Fact The Eurasian water shrew has special water-resistant fur that captures air bubbles as it enters the water. This allows them to be incredibly buoyant.

Conservation status — Least concern

Mammals
Placental mammals
Shrews and their relatives

European Mole
Talpa europaea

Factfile

Habitat	Underground in fields, woodland, pasture
Distribution	Europe
Size	4.5 to 6 in long
Weight	2.5 to 4.5 oz
Life span	2 to 3 years
Predators	Owls, buzzards, herons, cats, dogs

Diet European moles feed mainly on worms, but they will also eat a variety of other invertebrates, small soil animals and the occasional snake or lizard.

Fact When there are lots of earthworms the European mole will bite and paralyze them. They will be stored in a chamber for the mole to eat later.

Conservation status — **Least concern**

Aardvark
Orycteropus afer

| Mammals |
| Placental mammals |
| Aardvarks |

Factfile

Habitat	Grassland, savannah
Distribution	Sub-Saharan Africa
Size	3.5 to 5.5 ft long
Weight	88 to 180 lb
Life span	Up to 18 years
Predators	Lions, leopards, hyenas, pythons

Diet Aardvarks eat ants and termites. They use their claws to dig into anthills and termite mounds, and use their long tongues to reach the insects.

Fact The aardvark's wormlike tongue can be up to 12 inches long and is sticky so it can trap as many as 50,000 termites and ants in one night!

Conservation status   **Least concern**

Mammals
Placental mammals
Hyraxes

Rock Hyrax
Procavia capensis

Factfile

Habitat	Dry savannah, rain forest
Distribution	Eastern to southern Africa
Size	15 to 22 in long
Weight	6.5 to 9 lb
Life span	5 to 12 years
Predators	Leopards, large birds, snakes

Diet Rock hyraxes feast on many different types of plant matter. Grasses make up 78% of their diet during wet seasons, but only 57% during dry seasons.

Fact The hyrax's closest relative is the elephant. They have similar teeth, toes and skulls. Hyraxes have two large incisor teeth that form tiny tusks.

Conservation status — **Least concern**

African Bush Elephant
Loxodonta africana

Mammals
Placental mammals
Elephants

Factfile

Habitat	Forest, savannah, flood plains
Distribution	Central and southern Africa
Size	10 to 12 ft tall
Weight	4 to 6 tons
Life span	60 to 70 years
Predators	Humans, lions, hyenas (young only)

Diet Bush elephants eat leaves, roots, bark, grasses and fruit. Each day they can consume between 200 to 600 pounds of food and drink up to 50 gallons of water.

Fact They can create water holes by digging in dry riverbeds. They coat themselves with mud, which acts as protection from the sun and parasites.

Conservation status — **Vulnerable**

Mammals
Placental mammals
Elephants

African Forest Elephant
Loxodonta cyclotis

Factfile

Habitat   Forest, savannah, flood plains
Distribution   Central and southern Africa
Size   5.5 to 9.5 ft tall
Weight   3 to 6 tons
Life span   60 to 70 years
Predators   Lions and hyenas (young only)

Diet   The African forest elephant is a herbivore. Its diet consists mainly of leaves, fruit and tree bark, with occasional visits to mineral licks.

Fact   Although the African forest elephant is slightly smaller than the bush elephant, it is still one of the largest animals found on land today.

Conservation status: Endangered

Asiatic Elephant
Elephas maximus

Mammals
Placental mammals
Elephants

Factfile

Habitat	Rain forest, tropical woodland
Distribution	Indian subcontinent and Southeast Asia
Size	6.5 to 10 ft tall
Weight	3 to 5.5 tons
Life span	55 to 70 years
Predators	Tigers

Diet Asiatic elephants feed on grasses, fruit, roots, palm leaves, tree bark, shrubs and stems. These elephants eat up to 375 pounds of food each day.

Fact Asiatic elephants communicate via rumbles, bellows and moans. They are also able to emit low-frequency sounds that can travel several miles.

Conservation status: Endangered

Mammals

Placental mammals

Armadillos, sloths and pangolins

Nine-banded Armadillo
Dasypus novemcinctus

Factfile

Habitat Forest, scrubland
Distribution South, Central and North America
Size 24 to 32 in long
Weight 8 to 17 lb
Life span 7 to 20 years
Predators Alligators, bears, wild cats

Diet The armadillo's diet is mostly made up of insects, grubs and worms. It will sometimes eat fruit, amphibians, small reptiles, and birds' eggs.

Fact The scaly plates that cover its head, body and tail are called scutes. The nine jointed bands on its midsection allow the armadillo to bend.

Conservation status | **Least concern**

Brown-throated Sloth
Bradypus variegatus

	Mammals
	Placental mammals
	Armadillos, sloths and pangolins

Factfile

Habitat — Tropical forest
Distribution — South America, southern Central America
Size — 24 in long
Weight — 8 to 12 lb
Life span — 30 to 40 years
Predators — Spectacled owls, harpy eagles

Diet — The brown-throated sloth is a strict herbivore. It consumes various parts of dioecious trees, including leaves, flowers, and fruits.

Fact — The fur of these slow-moving creatures is an ideal place for algae to breed. This makes their coats green, which acts as camouflage.

Conservation status: Least concern

Mammals
Placental mammals
Armadillos, sloths and pangolins

Giant Pangolin
Manis gigantea

Factfile

Habitat	Forest, savannah
Distribution	Africa
Size	4 to 4.5 ft long
Weight	Up to 73 lb
Life span	Estimated at 20 years
Predators	Leopards, hyenas

Diet The giant pangolin eats termites and ants. It uses its claws to tear open the nests and its long, sticky tongue to probe the cracks for insects.

Fact When startled it hides its head between its front legs, showing only its strongly armored shoulders. If it is touched it rolls up into a ball.

Conservation status — **Near threatened**

European Hare
Lepus europaeus

Mammals
Placental mammals
Rabbits, hares and pikas

Factfile

Habitat	Forest, mountainous regions
Distribution	Europe and North America
Size	24 to 30 in long
Weight	6.5 to 11 lb
Life span	Up to 12 years
Predators	Foxes, wolves, wild cats, hawks, owls

Diet The European hare's diet consists mainly of grasses in summer and herbs in winter. This hare will also eat some buds, twigs and tree bark.

Fact Their long hind legs and sleek bodies are built for speed. They can run at 35 miles per hour and outrun most predators by running in a zigzag fashion.

Conservation status — Least concern

Mammals
Placental mammals
Rabbits, hares and pikas

European Rabbit
Oryctolagus cuniculus

Factfile

Habitat	Brushy fields, forest, urban areas
Distribution	Every continent except Asia and Antarctica
Size	15 to 20 in long
Weight	3 to 5.5 lb
Life span	1 to 9 years
Predators	Dogs, cats, mustelids, hawks, owls

Diet The European rabbit's diet includes grasses, leaves, buds, tree bark and roots. They will eat crops of lettuce, cabbage, root vegetables and grains.

Fact These rabbits originate from Spain, northwestern Africa and Portugal. They now live throughout the world (except in Asia and Antarctica).

Conservation status — **Least concern**

Eastern Cottontail
Sylvilagus floridanus

Mammals
Placental mammals
Rabbits, hares and pikas

Factfile

Habitat	Desert, swamp and hardwood forest
Distribution	North and South America
Size	16 to 19 in long
Weight	2 to 3 lb
Life span	1 to 3 years
Predators	Hawks, owls, red foxes, coyotes, weasels

Diet Cottontails eat grass, clover, fruits and some vegetables. In the winter they feed on the woody parts of plants such as twigs and bark.

Fact During the summer they have short brown fur and in the winter the fur becomes longer and grayer. All year long the underside of the tail is white.

Conservation status — Least concern

Mammals
Placental mammals
Rabbits, hares and pikas

American Pika
Ochotona princeps

Factfile

Habitat   Broken rock fields fringed by alpine meadows
Distribution Western North America
Size   6 to 9 in long
Weight   4 to 6 oz
Life span   2 to 7 years
Predators   Bobcats, coyotes, weasels, foxes, eagles

Diet American pikas are plant eaters. Their diet mainly consists of green grasses, but they will also eat some thistles, moss, lichen and sedges.

Fact During late summer pikas collect vegetation and store it to eat later. This is called "haying" and helps them survive the harsh winters.

Conservation status   **Least concern**

Eurasian Beaver
Castor fiber

| Mammals |
| Placental mammals |
| Rodents |

Factfile

Habitat	Lakes, ponds, rivers, streams
Distribution	Asia, Europe
Size	2.5 to 4 ft long
Weight	24 to 66 lb
Life span	15 to 20 years
Predators	Wolves, bears, foxes

Diet This beaver mostly eats tree bark and cambium, the soft tissue that grows under the bark, but they will eat roots, buds and water plants.

Fact Beavers have long sharp upper and lower teeth, which they use to cut into trees and vegetation. These teeth grow throughout the beaver's life.

Conservation status — Least concern

Mammals
Placental mammals
Rodents

Capybara
Hydrochoerus hydrochaeris

Factfile

Habitat	Dense vegetation close to fresh water
Distribution	Central and South America
Size	3.5 to 4.5 ft long
Weight	77 to 146 lb
Life span	8 to 10 years
Predators	Jaguars, caimans, harpy eagles

Diet Capybara are herbivores who mainly eat grasses and aquatic plants, but also eat tree bark, grains, squashes and occasionally some fruit.

Fact The capybara is semiaquatic. They have webbed toes that help them swim. They sometimes hide in water with only their noses sticking out!

Conservation status — **Least concern**

Alpine Marmot
Marmota marmota

| Mammals |
| Placental mammals |
| Rodents |

Factfile

Habitat	Mountainous grassland
Distribution	Alpine mountains of Europe
Size	18 to 27 in long
Weight	6 to 9 lb
Life span	Up to 15 years
Predators	Foxes, golden eagles

Diet The alpine marmot is mostly vegetarian. They eat grass, flowers, bulbs and seeds, but will supplement their diet with insects and birds' eggs.

Fact During good weather the alpine marmot eats as much as possible, laying down fat for the winter. They use this stored fat during their hibernation.

Conservation status — Least concern

Mammals

Placental mammals

Rodents

Eastern Gray Squirrel
Sciurus carolinensis

Factfile

Habitat	Woodland, forest
Distribution	North America
Size	15 to 20 in long
Weight	12 to 26 oz
Life span	10 to 12 years
Predators	Weasels, foxes, wolves, cats, birds of prey

Diet The Eastern gray squirrel feeds on tree bark, seeds, walnuts, acorns and other kinds of nuts, and the various fungi that are found in the forest.

Fact They are scatter-hoarders like other rodents. They hide huge quantities of food for later. They can hide thousands of items of food each year.

Conservation status — **Least concern**

Eurasian Red Squirrel
Sciurus vulgaris

Mammals

Placental mammals

Rodents

Factfile

Habitat	Deciduous and coniferous forest
Distribution	Europe and northern Asia
Size	7.5 to 9 in long
Weight	Up to 1.4 lb
Life span	2 to 7 years
Predators	Birds of prey, various mustelids

Diet The red squirrel's diet is mostly made up of seeds. They also eat some fungi, shoots and fruits of shrubs and trees, and occasionally birds' eggs.

Fact Red squirrels build nests, called dreys, often in the forks of tree trunks. They are solitary, but share dreys to keep warm in the cold winter.

Conservation status — **Least concern**

Mammals
Placental mammals
Primates

Greater Slow Loris
Nycticebus coucang

Factfile

Habitat	Tropical forest
Distribution	Indonesia, Malaysia, Thailand, Singapore
Size	11 to 15 in long
Weight	21 to 24 oz
Life span	Up to 20 years
Predators	Pythons, hawk-eagles, orangutans

Diet The greater slow loris has a varied diet. It feeds on saps, gums, nectars, stems, fruits, and occasionally arthropods such as spiders and insects.

Fact The loris can take toxins, from a gland on the side of the elbow, into its mouth and mix it with saliva. This gives it a deadly poisonous bite.

Conservation status — **Vulnerable**

Ring-tailed Lemur
Lemur catta

Mammals

Placental mammals

Primates

Factfile

Habitat	Dry forest, tropical jungle
Distribution	Madagascar
Size	15 to 18 in long
Weight	5 to 8 lb
Life span	Up to 27 years
Predators	Domestic dogs, raptors, fossas

Diet The ring-tailed lemur forages for fruit, which makes up the greater part of its diet, but it also eats leaves, flowers, tree bark and sap.

Fact Male ring-tailed lemurs compete for females by having stink fights! They smear scent on their tails and waft the smell towards their opponent.

Conservation status: Near threatened

Mammals
Placental mammals
Primates

Verreaux's Sifaka
Propithecus verreauxi

Factfile

Habitat	Deciduous and evergreen forest
Distribution	Madagascar
Size	18 to 22 in long
Weight	6.5 to 15.5 lb
Life span	Estimated at 15 years
Predators	Domestic dogs, fossas, harrier hawks

Diet Verreaux's sifakas are herbivorous and feed mostly on leaves, bark and flowers. When there is plenty of fruit they will include it in their diet.

Fact They can't walk easily on the ground because their bodies are designed for leaping through the trees, so they have to hop from side to side.

Conservation status: Vulnerable

Indri
Indri indri

	Mammals
	Placental mammals
	Primates

Factfile

Habitat	Lowland rain forest
Distribution	Eastern Madagascar
Size	2 to 2.5 ft tall
Weight	13 to 21 lb
Life span	15 to 22 years
Predators	Fossas, hawks, snakes

Diet The indri is primarily folivorous, which means it eats leaves. It prefers young, tender leaves but will also eat some seeds, fruits and flowers.

Fact These tree-dwelling animals cannot walk on all fours on the ground, so they stand upright, with arms outstretched and skip through the forest!

Conservation status: Endangered

Mammals
Placental mammals
Primates

Red Howler Monkey
Alouatta seniculus

Factfile

Habitat   Forest, rain forest
Distribution South America
Size   18 to 28 in long
Weight   10 to 14 lb
Life span   Up to 25 years
Predators   Jaguars

Diet The red howler monkey's diet mainly consists of leaves, but they also rely on nuts, small animals, fruits, flowers and seeds for important nutrients.

Fact These noisy monkeys are famous for their "dawn chorus." Their roaring and howling calls can be heard each morning in the forest up to 3 miles away.

Conservation status — **Least concern**

Black Spider Monkey
Ateles paniscus

| Mammals |
| Placental mammals |
| Primates |

Factfile

Habitat   Dense forest
Distribution South America
Size   16 to 24 in long
Weight   17.5 to 20 lb
Life span   20 years
Predators   Jaguars, pumas, ocelots, harpy eagles

Diet The black spider monkey feeds mainly on fruit and nuts but will also eat leaves, seeds, flower buds, birds' eggs, insects and some spiders.

Fact They have very long arms and hook-like hands with elongated fingers that allow them to swing through trees using a hand-over-hand motion.

Conservation status: Vulnerable

Mammals
Placental mammals
Primates

Emperor Tamarin
Saguinus imperator

Factfile

Habitat Lowland tropical forest
Distribution South America
Size 9 to 10.5 in long
Weight 10 to 16 oz
Life span 8 to 15 years
Predators Hawks, snakes, wild cats

Diet Tamarins eat fruit throughout the wet season. During the dry season they feed on a diet of nectar, fruits, flowers, ants and the occasional snail.

Fact They are known as "emperor" tamarins because of their white moustache that is said to resemble that of the German Emperor Wilhelm.

Conservation status: Least concern

Golden Lion Tamarin
Leontopithecus rosalia

Mammals

Placental mammals

Primates

Factfile

Habitat	Lowland tropical forest
Distribution	Brazil
Size	8 to 14 in long
Weight	1 to 1.5 lb
Life span	8 to 15 years
Predators	Hawks, wild cats, snakes, rats

Diet Golden lion tamarins feed on fruits, insects and small lizards. They search crevices, bark, plants and other hiding places for their prey.

Fact Tamarins groom each other much like many other primates do. They spend a lot of their time grooming and huddling together in groups.

Conservation status: Endangered

Mammals
Placental mammals
Primates

Olive Baboon
Papio anubis

Factfile

Habitat	Savannah, grassland steppe, rain forest
Distribution	Central sub-Saharan Africa
Size	1.5 to 2.5 ft long
Weight	31 to 55 lb
Life span	25 to 30 years
Predators	Leopards, chimpanzees

Diet Olive baboons are omnivores. They feed on grass, seeds, leaves, cereals, fruit, tubers, small mammals, invertebrates and some young birds.

Fact They communicate through facial expressions and vocal sounds. Over 30 baboon noises such as grunts, barks and screams have been recorded.

Conservation status Least concern

Proboscis Monkey
Nasalis larvatus

Mammals
Placental mammals
Primates

Factfile

Habitat Coastal mangrove, riverine forest
Distribution Borneo
Size 21 to 30 in tall
Weight 15 to 49 lb
Life span 15 to 20 years
Predators Clouded leopards, crocodiles

Diet The proboscis monkey feeds on mostly leaves between June and December, and then fruit from January to May. Seeds and flowers are also eaten.

Fact As well as using its nose to attract a mate, the male monkey can make his nose swell up to amplify its warning calls when threatened.

Conservation status **Endangered**

Mammals
Placental mammals
Primates

Common Chimpanzee
Pan troglodytes

Factfile

Habitat   Tropical forest, woody savannah
Distribution Western and Central Africa
Size   3.5 to 5.5 ft tall
Weight   55 to 154 lb
Life span   50 to 60 years
Predators   Leopards, snakes

Diet Chimpanzees mostly eat fruit and plants, but they also eat insects, eggs and meat. Their varied diet includes hundreds of different foods.

Fact Chimpanzees are closely related to other great apes such as orangutans and gorillas. They also share 98% of the same DNA as humans.

Conservation status: Endangered

Western Lowland Gorilla
Gorilla gorilla

Mammals
Placental mammals
Primates

Factfile

Habitat	Rain forest, dense jungle
Distribution	Central Africa
Size	4.5 to 5.5 ft tall
Weight	160 to 400 lb
Life span	25 to 50 years
Predators	Leopards, crocodiles

Diet Gorillas mainly eat pith, shoots and leaves. Fruits are also an important food source. Over 100 fruit species have been recorded in their diet.

Fact The intimidating chest beating of a male gorilla is usually used to scare off intruders while the rest of his troop disappears into the forest.

Conservation status: Critically endangered

Mammals
Placental mammals
Primates

Bornean Orangutan
Pongo pygmaeus

Factfile

Habitat	Lowland forest, peat swamp
Distribution	Borneo
Size	4 to 5 ft tall
Weight	75 to 200 lb
Life span	30 to 40 years
Predators	Tigers, clouded leopards

Diet Over half of an orangutan's diet is made up of fruit (mainly figs). They also eat leaves, bark, flowers, nuts, insects and small mammals.

Fact Bornean orangutans generally live alone in the wild. The adult males communicate with each other using a vocalization called a long call.

Conservation status: Endangered

Black Flying Fox
Pteropus alecto

Mammals
Placental mammals
Bats

Factfile

Habitat	Forest, rain forest, savannah, woodland
Distribution	Australia and some parts of Asia
Size	9 to 11 in long
Weight	1.3 to 2 lb
Life span	Up to 5 years
Predators	Birds of prey

Diet The black flying fox has a varied diet. They are known to feed on the fruits, pollen and nectar of over 20 different rain forest plants.

Fact Flying foxes are the only known animals that pollinate some rain forest plant species. These bats play a vital role in keeping the rain forests healthy.

Conservation status: Least concern

Mammals
Placental mammals
Hedgehogs

European Hedgehog
Erinaceus europaeus

Factfile

Habitat	Fields, hedgerows, urban areas
Distribution	Europe, central Asia
Size	5 to 6.5 in long
Weight	1.5 to 2.5 lb
Life span	5 to 8 years
Predators	Dogs, foxes, snakes, large owls, badgers

Diet Hedgehogs have a diet of slugs, snails, earthworms, beetles and earwigs. They will sometimes eat larger animals such as frogs, mice and chicks.

Fact During hibernation the hedgehog's body temperature drops as low as 40° F and the heart rate drops from 190 to about 20 beats per minute.

Conservation status — Least concern

Arctic Fox
Vulpes lagopus

Mammals

Placental mammals

Dogs and relatives

Factfile

Habitat	Polar forest regions
Distribution	Arctic regions
Size	28 to 44 in long
Weight	6 to 20 lb
Life span	7 to 10 years
Predators	Snowy owls, wolves, polar bears

Diet The Arctic fox tends to prey on lemmings, hares, reptiles, amphibians and occasionally vulnerable seal pups that are separated from their herd.

Fact As they spend a great deal of time in the cold snow, Arctic foxes have extremely thick fur, which is believed to be the warmest fur of all mammals.

Conservation status — **Least concern**

Mammals
Placental mammals
Dogs and relatives

Red Fox
Vulpes vulpes

Factfile

Habitat Forest, desert, mountains, urban areas
Distribution Throughout most of the northern hemisphere
Size 18 to 35 in long
Weight 6.5 to 30 lb
Life span 3 to 4 years in the wild
Predators Eagles, coyotes, gray wolves, bears, humans

Diet Foxes are omnivores, eating plants and animals. Their varied diet includes rabbits, snakes, insects, birds, mice, berries, grasses and fruits.

Fact Many red foxes have taken to living in urban areas. In towns much of their diet consists of food they have scavenged, mainly from trash.

Conservation status — **Least concern**

Fennec Fox
Vulpes zerda

Mammals
Placental mammals
Dogs and relatives

Factfile

Habitat	Desert, mountain areas
Distribution	Central Sahara and surrounding areas
Size	12 to 16 in long
Weight	1.5 to 3 lb
Life span	Up to 10 years
Predators	Eagle-owls, caracals, jackals, hyenas

Diet The fennec fox eats a variety of plants, small rodents, birds, eggs, lizards and insects. They can also hunt larger mammals such as desert hares.

Fact The fennec is the smallest of all foxes but has the largest proportioned ears. The ears radiate heat from the body and keep the fennec cool.

Conservation status: Least concern

- Mammals
- Placental mammals
- Dogs and relatives

Raccoon Dog
Nyctereutes procyonoides

Factfile

Habitat	Thick forest close to water
Distribution	Eastern Asia, Europe
Size	19 to 25 in long
Weight	8 to 22 lb
Life span	3 to 8 years
Predators	Foxes, wolves, wildcats

Diet Raccoon dogs spend a great deal of time close to water, so their diet consists of frogs, fish, rodents, small birds, eggs, insects and spiders.

Fact Raccoon dogs have dexterous front paws that come in very handy when trying to catch slippery food in the water and when climbing trees.

Conservation status: Least concern

Maned Wolf
Chrysocyon brachyurus

Mammals
Placental mammals
Dogs and relatives

Factfile

Habitat	Grassland, savannah, dry shrub forest, swamp
Distribution	South America
Size	4 to 4.5 ft long
Weight	44 to 51 lb
Life span	Up to 13 years
Predators	No natural predators

Diet These omnivorous animals eat a wide variety of plants, fruits and small animals, including birds, reptiles, rodents and small mammals.

Fact The maned wolf gets its name from the distinctive black mane of fur along its neck. This mane will stand erect when the wolf senses danger.

Conservation status — **Near threatened**

Mammals
Placental mammals
Dogs and relatives

Arctic Wolf
Canis lupus arctos

Factfile

Habitat	Grass plains, tundra forest
Distribution	Arctic Circle
Size	3 to 5 ft long
Weight	65 to 175 lb
Life span	7 to 10 years
Predators	Polar bears, other wolves

Diet The main prey of the Arctic wolf are musk ox and arctic hare, but they will also sometimes hunt and eat caribou, lemmings, seals and nesting birds.

Fact Arctic wolves can survive the harsh conditions and subzero temperatures of the Arctic. Each year they spend five months in total darkness.

Conservation status — **Least concern**

Dingo
Canis lupus dingo

Mammals
Placental mammals
Dogs and relatives

Factfile

Habitat	Desert, wet and dry forest
Distribution	Australia, Southeast Asia
Size	3 to 4 ft long
Weight	28 to 44 lb
Life span	7 to 15 years
Predators	Large reptiles

Diet The dingo has a similar diet to other pack canines such as wolves. They eat rodents, small mammals, lizards, birds, wallabies and even kangaroos.

Fact Dingoes may live alone or in packs of up to ten animals. They roam great distances and communicate with each other through wolflike howls.

Conservation status — **Vulnerable**

Mammals
Placental mammals
Dogs and relatives

Coyote
Canis latrans

Factfile

Habitat	Forest, plains, desert
Distribution	North and Central America
Size	2.5 to 3 ft long
Weight	15 to 45 lb
Life span	Up to 15 years
Predators	Bears, wolves

Diet Coyotes eat small mammals such as voles, prairie dogs, eastern cottontails and mice. They will also eat birds, snakes, lizards and invertebrates.

Fact Coyotes have an amazing sense of smell that they use for hunting. They can even detect prey that is scurrying below the snow.

Conservation status — **Least concern**

African Wild Dog
Lycaon pictus

Mammals

Placental mammals

Dogs and relatives

Factfile

Habitat	Open plains, savannah
Distribution	Sub-Saharan Africa
Size	2.5 to 3.5 ft long
Weight	37.5 to 80 lb
Life span	10 to 13 years
Predators	Lions, hyenas

Diet African wild dogs mostly prey on large mammals such as warthogs and antelopes. They will also eat rodents, lizards, birds and insects.

Fact African wild dogs live in packs of around 10 members. All of the members help to care for the young. A litter may contain as many as 16 pups.

Conservation status: Endangered

- Mammals
- Placental mammals
- Bears

Polar Bear
Ursus maritimus

Factfile

Habitat	Coastal ice fields, floating ice
Distribution	The Arctic
Size	6 to 8 ft long
Weight	330 to 1700 lb
Life span	20 to 30 years
Predators	No natural predators

Diet The polar bear is the largest carnivorous mammal on land. The skins and blubber of ringed seals make up the bulk of the polar bear's diet.

Fact Polar bears have wide front paws with slightly webbed toes that help them swim. They paddle with their front feet and steer with their hind feet.

Conservation status: Vulnerable

American Black Bear
Ursus americanus

Mammals
Placental mammals
Bears

Factfile

Habitat	Forest, woodland
Distribution	North America
Size	4 to 6 ft long
Weight	220 to 600 lb
Life span	15 to 30 years
Predators	Humans, wolves, pumas

Diet Black bears forage for fruits and nuts in the trees, along with eating grasses, roots, bulbs and small animals such as insects or rodents.

Fact American black bears will stand up on their hind legs to make themselves look even bigger in an attempt to intimidate a predator or a rival.

Conservation status — **Least concern**

Mammals
Placental mammals
Bears

Asiatic Black Bear
Ursus thibetanus

Factfile

Habitat	Deciduous tropical forest
Distribution	Central and southern Asia, Russia, Japan
Size	4 to 6 ft long
Weight	150 to 400 lb
Life span	15 to 25 years
Predators	Tigers, wolves

Diet Asiatic black bears forage for nuts, seeds, fruits, shoots, leaves, grasses, herbs, grubs and insects. They will also eat some birds and rodents.

Fact Asiatic black bears have poor sight and hearing like other bears. They have to rely heavily on their sense of smell to figure out their surroundings.

Conservation status — **Endangered**

Brown Bear
Ursus arctos

Mammals

Placental mammals

Bears

Factfile

Habitat	Forest
Distribution	North America, Eurasia
Size	5 to 9 ft long
Weight	175 to 1300 lb
Life span	20 to 30 years
Predators	Humans, wolves, cougars

Diet Brown bears will eat almost anything, from leaves and berries, bugs and insects to rodents, squirrels and sheep. They are fond of salmon.

Fact Brown bears can climb trees to eat or escape predators, but only when they are cubs! As adults they become far too heavy for climbing.

Conservation status: Endangered

Mammals
Placental mammals
Bears

Giant Panda
Ailuropoda melanoleuca

Factfile

Habitat	High-altitude moist bamboo forest
Distribution	Mountains of central China
Size	5 to 6 ft long
Weight	175 to 350 lb
Life span	20 to 30 years
Predators	Humans, leopards (young only)

Diet A giant panda's diet is about 99% bamboo. The balance consists of other grasses and occasional small rodents or musk deer fawns.

Fact Bamboo is low in nutrients, so pandas spend up to 16 hours a day foraging and eating. The rest of their time is spent mostly sleeping and resting.

Conservation status | **Endangered**

California Sea Lion
Zalophus californianus

Mammals

Placental mammals

Sea lions, walruses and seals

Factfile

Habitat	Coastline
Distribution	America, Galápagos Islands, Sea of Japan
Size	5.5 to 7.5 ft long
Weight	550 to 800 lb
Life span	Up to 17 years
Predators	Great white sharks, bull sharks, orcas

Diet Sea lions are opportunistic feeders, who eat a diet including anchovies, mackerel and rockfish. They also eat squid and octopuses.

Fact Sea lions get their name from the loud roars they produce. Males of some sea lion species even grow thick manes around their necks.

Conservation status — Least concern

Mammals
Placental mammals
Sea lions, walruses and seals

Walrus
Odobenus rosmarus

Factfile

Habitat Ice floes, remote rocky coastlines
Distribution Arctic Circle
Size 7 to 11 ft long
Weight Up to 1.5 tons
Life span 30 to 40 years
Predators Orcas, polar bears

Diet Walruses feed on a variety of different prey species including clams, snails, worms, squid, octopuses and even some species of slow-moving fish.

Fact Walruses use their huge tusks to fight each other, to defend against predators and to haul their massive bodies out of the ocean and onto the ice.

Conservation status Near threatened

Gray Seal
Halichoerus grypus

Mammals

Placental mammals

Sea lions, walruses and seals

Factfile

Habitat	Cool waters, rocky shores
Distribution	Europe, North America, Russia
Size	6 to 7.5 ft long
Weight	330 to 500 lb
Life span	18 to 25 years
Predators	Humans, sharks, orcas

Diet Gray seals eat fish and occasionally crustaceans and mollusks. At least 29 species of fish have been recorded as being eaten by these seals.

Fact These seals swallow small fish whole. Large fish are brought to the surface, where their heads are bitten off and then their bodies eaten.

Conservation status — **Least concern**

Mammals
Placental mammals
Sea lions, walruses and seals

Leopard Seal
Hydrurga leptonyx

Factfile

Habitat Cold waters
Distribution Southern hemisphere
Size 7.5 to 10.5 ft long
Weight 440 to 1300 lb
Life span 20 to 24 years
Predators Sharks, orcas

Diet Leopard seals eat almost any animal, including penguins, fish, squid, crustaceans, and even the pups of crabeater, Weddell and fur seals.

Fact Female leopard seals gives birth to pups in a hole they have dug in the ice. It can take them several months to complete digging this icy den.

Conservation status — Least concern

Northern Raccoon
Procyon lotor

Mammals
Placental mammals
Raccoons and relatives

Factfile

Habitat	Woodland areas close to water
Distribution	North and South America, Asia, Europe
Size	23 to 37 in long
Weight	4 to 23 lb
Life span	12 to 16 years
Predators	Bobcats, foxes, wolves, pumas

Diet Raccoons will eat whatever they can get. Plants make up most of a raccoon's diet, but they will also eat invertebrates such as insects and crayfish.

Fact It is easy to identify raccoon tracks in mud because the raccoon's front paws have five toes that look very similar to small human hands.

Conservation status — Least concern

Mammals
Placental mammals
Raccoons and relatives

Red Panda
Ailurus fulgens

Factfile

Habitat	High-altitude mountain forest
Distribution	Himalayas
Size	20 to 26 in long
Weight	6.5 to 13.5 lb
Life span	8 to 12 years
Predators	Snow leopards, martens

Diet Red pandas primarily eat bamboo leaves and fresh shoots. They will also feed on berries, blossoms, birds' eggs and various plants' small leaves.

Fact Red pandas typically live alone, but sometimes form pairs or small groups. They are most active at dusk and dawn, when they forage for food.

Conservation status — **Endangered**

Meerkat
Suricata suricatta

Mammals

Placental mammals

Raccoons and relatives

Factfile

Habitat	Semidesert, scrubland
Distribution	Southwestern Africa
Size	10 to 14 in long
Weight	1 to 2 lb
Life span	10 to 14 years
Predators	Hawks, jackals, snakes

Diet A meerkat's diet consists mostly of insects, grubs, birds' eggs, small reptiles and the occasional scorpion (meerkats are immune to their venom).

Fact Meerkats live in groups as large as 40. They will work together to gather food, keep a look out for predators, and take care of the babies.

Conservation status — **Least concern**

- Mammals
- Placental mammals
- Raccoons and relatives

Striped Skunk
Mephitis mephitis

Factfile

Habitat   Open woodland, dense shrub
Distribution North America
Size   16 to 31 in long
Weight   1.5 to 14 lb
Life span   5 to 8 years
Predators   Owls, coyotes, wild cats

Diet Striped skunks eat insects, nuts, fish, small vertebrates, fruits, grasses, fungi, berries and eggs. They will also eat the carcasses of dead animals.

Fact The skunk is famous for its ability to spray a foul-smelling liquid at potential attackers. The spray is so strong it can blind predators temporarily.

Conservation status: Least concern

Stoat
Mustela erminea

- Mammals
- Placental mammals
- Raccoons and relatives

Factfile

Habitat	Moorland, woodland
Distribution	Europe, Asia, North America
Size	10 to 14 in long
Weight	.5 to 1 lb
Life span	4 to 6 years
Predators	Foxes, snakes, wild cats

Diet Stoats eat rodents, fish, eggs, insects, small reptiles and amphibians. Despite being smaller than a rabbit, the stoat still hunts and kills them.

Fact Although the stoat's coat is brown in summer, it sometimes turns pure white in the winter, except for the tip of the tail, which remains black.

Conservation status — **Least concern**

Mammals
Placental mammals
Raccoons and relatives

Wolverine
Gulo gulo

Factfile

Habitat	Mountainous regions and dense forest
Distribution	Europe, North America and the Arctic Circle
Size	2 to 3 ft long
Weight	22 to 68 lb
Life span	10 to 15 years
Predators	Humans, wolves, bears

Diet Wolverines mostly eat rabbits and rodents, but will attack an animal many times their size, such as caribou, if it appears weak or injured.

Fact The wolverine has extremely powerful jaws that can crush large bones. A wolverine's jaws are strong enough to chew through a chain-link fence!

Conservation status — **Least concern**

Eurasian Badger
Meles meles

Mammals

Placental mammals

Raccoons and relatives

Factfile

Habitat	Woodland, grassland, semidesert
Distribution	Europe, Asia, Africa
Size	22 to 35 in long
Weight	14 to 37 lb
Life span	6 to 14 years
Predators	Wolves, lynx, bears

Diet Eurasian badgers are omnivores and they mainly feed on earthworms, insects, frogs, birds, lizards, small mammals, fruit, eggs and carrion.

Fact Some of the burrows that Eurasian badgers live in are believed to be at least 100 years old. Some badger tunnels can measure over 300 yards long.

Conservation status — **Least concern**

Mammals
Placental mammals
Raccoons and relatives

Honey Badger
Mellivora capensis

Factfile

Habitat	Arid grassland, savannah, rain forest
Distribution	Africa, the Middle East, India
Size	Up to 32 in long
Weight	20 to 26 lb
Life span	Up to 26 years
Predators	Lions, leopards

Diet The honey badger is a fierce predator that will attack and eat snakes, reptiles, rodents and birds. It has even been known to attack the African buffalo.

Fact Honey badgers often attack beehives to eat the honey and larval bees. Bees may sting them many times, but their thick skin protects them.

Conservation status — **Least concern**

Sea Otter
Enhydra lutris

Mammals

Placental mammals

Raccoons and relatives

Factfile

Habitat	Unpolluted areas close to the shore
Distribution	Russia, North America, Japan
Size	3 to 5 ft long
Weight	30 to 100 lb
Life span	12 to 15 years
Predators	Sharks, orcas

Diet A sea otter's diet includes slow-moving fish and marine invertebrates including crabs, sea urchins, abalone, clams, mussels and snails.

Fact Sea otters are the only otters to give birth in the water. Mothers usually have one pup and nurture their young while floating on their backs.

Conservation status — **Endangered**

Mammals
Placental mammals
Raccoons and relatives

Northern River Otter
Lontra canadensis

Factfile

Habitat	Riverbanks, lakes, streams
Distribution	North America
Size	30 to 50 in long
Weight	11 to 33 lb
Life span	8 to 21 years
Predators	Birds, foxes, wolves

Diet Northern river otters eat aquatic animals such as amphibians, invertebrates, fish and some turtles. They also eat birds and small mammals.

Fact These otters have water-repellent fur to keep them dry and warm when they are in water. Their ears and nostrils close when they are submerged.

Conservation status — **Near threatened**

Fishing Cat
Prionailurus viverrinus

Mammals
Placental mammals
Cats and relatives

Factfile

Habitat	Variety of wetland habitats
Distribution	Southeast Asia
Size	22 to 35 in long
Weight	12 to 18 lb
Life span	10 to 12 years
Predators	No known predators

Diet Fishing cats eat birds, small mammals, snakes, snails and fish. They hunt by tapping the water's surface with a paw to attract fish, then diving in.

Fact When in the water, the fishing cat may use its flattened, short tail like the rudder of a boat. This helps to control its direction through the water.

Conservation status **Endangered**

Mammals
Placental mammals
Cats and relatives

Iberian Lynx
Lynx pardinus

Factfile

Habitat Scrubland, grassland
Distribution Spain, Portugal
Size 2.5 to 4 ft long
Weight 24 to 33 lb
Life span Up to 13 years
Predators No natural predators

Diet The Iberian lynx has a diet mostly consisting of small mammals, such as rabbits and birds. When rabbits are scarce, it will hunt deer and wild sheep.

Fact There could be as few as 300 Iberian lynx left in the wild. Charities are breeding the lynx in captivity and reintroducing them into the wild.

Conservation status — Critically endangered

Bobcat
Lynx rufus

Mammals
Placental mammals
Cats and relatives

Factfile

Habitat Mountainous forest, swamp, desert
Distribution North America
Size 26 to 39 in long
Weight 9 to 22 lb
Life span 12 to 15 years
Predators Cougars, wolves, coyotes

Diet The bobcat eats a wide variety of small mammals such as rabbits, skunks, raccoons, moles and squirrels. It will also eat birds and reptiles.

Fact When walking, bobcats will place their back feet in the prints of their front feet. This enables them to be very quiet, which is ideal for stalking prey.

Conservation status — **Least concern**

Mammals
Placental mammals
Cats and relatives

Caracal
Caracal caracal

Factfile

Habitat	Dry woodland, savannah
Distribution	Africa, Asia
Size	2 to 3.5 ft long
Weight	14 to 44 lb
Life span	12 to 15 years
Predators	Hyenas, lions

Diet The caracal feeds on rodents, small antelope, hares and birds, and sometimes sheep and goats. It is mainly active in the mornings and evenings.

Fact The caracal's black ear tufts can grow up to 4 inches long. The tufts focus sound into the ears, improving the animal's ability to pinpoint potential prey.

Conservation status   **Least concern**

Ocelot
Leopardus pardalis

Mammals
Placental mammals
Cats and relatives

Factfile

Habitat	Tropical jungle, grassland, marsh
Distribution	South America
Size	25 to 39 in long
Weight	15 to 35 lb
Life span	8 to 12 years
Predators	Jaguars, pumas, harpy eagles

Diet The ocelot's diet consists of small animals like rats, mice and armadillos. They will also take on larger prey such as deer, anteaters and monkeys.

Fact The ocelot is the only small cat that sleeps lying down with its forepaws outstretched in front of its body and its head resting on them like a dog!

Conservation status — Least concern

Mammals
Placental mammals
Cats and relatives

Tiger
Panthera tigris

Factfile

Habitat	Forest, woodland, jungle, grassland
Distribution	South and East Asia
Size	5 to 11 ft long
Weight	200 to 700 lb
Life span	8 to 25 years
Predators	No natural predators

Diet Tigers eat a variety of prey from termites to elephant calves. Common prey includes moose, deer species, pigs, cows, buffalo and goats.

Fact Unlike most cats, tigers are strong swimmers and seem to enjoy the water. They enter rivers and lakes to chase prey or to cool themselves down.

Conservation status — **Endangered**

Puma
Puma concolor

Mammals

Placental mammals

Cats and relatives

Factfile

Habitat Mountain forests, jungles
Distribution North and South America
Size 3 to 5 ft long
Weight 65 to 230 lb
Life span 10 to 15 years
Predators Bears, wolves

Diet A puma's main diet is ungulates such as deer, horses, elk, cattle and sheep. It will eat any animal it can catch, even large animals such as moose.

Fact Although the puma is a fairly large cat it has many similar physical characteristics to small cats. The puma is the largest cat that has the ability to purr.

Conservation status — Least concern

Mammals
Placental mammals
Cats and relatives

Clouded Leopard
Neofelis nebulosa

Factfile

Habitat Dense tropical forest, jungle
Distribution Southeast Asia
Size 2 to 3.5 ft long
Weight 24 to 66 lb
Life span 11 to 17 years
Predators Tigers, leopards

Diet The diet of the clouded leopard is thought to include a variety of prey such as birds, squirrels, monkeys, deer and even some wild pigs.

Fact This leopard is skilled at climbing. It can hang upside down beneath branches, using its large paws and sharp claws to keep a good grip.

Conservation status: Vulnerable

Leopard
Panthera pardus

Mammals

Placental mammals

Cats and relatives

Factfile

Habitat	Rain forest, grassland, mountains
Distribution	Sub-Saharan Africa, southern Asia
Size	3 to 6 ft long
Weight	46 to 165 lb
Life span	10 to 15 years
Predators	Tigers, lions

Diet Leopards eat small hoofed mammals like gazelles, impalas, deer and wildebeest. On occasion, they may also hunt monkeys, rodents and birds.

Fact Leopards protect their food from other animals by dragging it up into trees. They will leave prey for days, returning again when they are hungry.

Conservation status — **Near threatened**

- Mammals
- Placental mammals
- Cats and relatives

Cheetah
Acinonyx jubatus

Factfile

Habitat	Open grassland
Distribution	Asia and Africa
Size	3.5 to 4.5 ft long
Weight	88 to 143 lb
Life span	6 to 12 years
Predators	Lions, eagles

Diet The cheetah eats antelopes such as Thompson's gazelles and impalas, the young of large antelopes, young warthogs, rabbits and birds.

Fact Cheetahs are the fastest animals on land and can reach speeds of 68 miles per hour, but can run only 400 to 600 yards before they are exhausted.

Conservation status: Vulnerable

Lion
Panthera leo

Mammals

Placental mammals

Cats and relatives

Factfile

Habitat	Open woodland, scrub, grassland
Distribution	Sub-Saharan Africa
Size	4.5 to 8 ft long
Weight	265 to 550 lb
Life span	8 to 18 years
Predators	No natural predators

Diet Hunting in packs means lions can take prey as large as wildebeest, zebras, buffalo, young elephants, rhinos, hippopotamuses and giraffes.

Fact Each lion pack (called a pride) has a specific area that it controls. A pride's territory can be as large as 160 miles of scrub, grassland and open woodland.

Conservation status — **Vulnerable**

Mammals
Placental mammals
Cats and relatives

Striped Hyena
Hyaena hyaena

Factfile

Habitat	Mountainous regions with scrub woodland
Distribution	Africa, the Middle East, India, Asia
Size	Up to 40 in long
Weight	55 to 100 lb
Life span	10 to 24 years
Predators	Lions, African wild dogs

Diet The striped hyena is mostly a scavenger. They feed on carrion but they also catch live prey such as insects, rodents, birds, lizards and rabbits.

Fact The hyena has a powerful digestive system. It consumes a wide range of animals and vegetation. It can even digest skin, teeth and bones.

Conservation status — **Near threatened**

Spotted Hyena
Crocuta crocuta

Mammals

Placental mammals

Cats and relatives

Factfile

Habitat	Savannah, scrubland
Distribution	Africa
Size	3 to 5 ft long
Weight	90 to 190 lb
Life span	20 to 25 years
Predators	Lions, leopards, crocodiles

Diet Spotted hyenas steal others' prey as well as hunt for their own. They hunt lizards, birds, snakes and large mammals such as antelope or wildebeest.

Fact Spotted hyenas can trot at 6 miles per hour for long distances. They can run as fast as 30 miles per hour and are also very strong swimmers.

Conservation status — **Least concern**

Mammals
Placental mammals
Hoofed mammals

Przewalski's Wild Horse
Equus ferus przewalskii

Factfile

Habitat Grassy desert, plains
Distribution Mongolia
Size Up to 7 ft long
Weight 440 to 660 lb
Life span 20 years (in captivity)
Predators Humans

Diet The diet of the Przewalski's horse is made up primarily of grass, but occasionally they will also eat some bark, leaves, fruits and roots.

Fact The Przewalski's horse became extinct in the wild during the 1960s due to hunting. In 2008 they began successfully being reintroduced to the wild.

Conservation status: Critically endangered

Burchell's Zebra
Equus burchellii

- Mammals
- Placental mammals
- Hoofed mammals

Factfile

Habitat	Open grassland, plains
Distribution	Sub-Saharan Africa
Size	6.5 to 8.5 ft long
Weight	400 to 850 lb
Life span	20 to 30 years
Predators	Lions, leopards, hyenas

Diet Zebras are herbivores that occasionally browse on herbs, leaves and twigs, but 90% of their diet comes from the stems and sheaths of grasses.

Fact At first glance zebras in a large herd might all look alike, but in fact a zebra's stripes are as unique as human fingerprints and help identify individuals.

Conservation status: Least concern

Mammals
Placental mammals
Hoofed mammals

Grevy's Zebra
Equus grevyi

Factfile

Habitat	Semiarid grassland
Distribution	Kenya, southern Ethiopia
Size	4 to 5 ft long
Weight	770 to 990 lb
Life span	12 to 13 years
Predators	Lions, cheetahs, hyenas, African wild dogs

Diet These zebras feed mainly on grasses, but also eat bark, fruit and leaves. They require a vast quantity of food, so spend about 60% of their day eating.

Fact The sleek coat of the Grevy's zebra is patterned with black and white vertical stripes that are much narrower than those of the Burchell's zebra.

Conservation status: Endangered

Black Rhinoceros
Diceros bicornis

Mammals
Placental mammals
Hoofed mammals

Factfile

Habitat Tropical bushland, grassland, savannah
Distribution Central and eastern Africa
Size 10 to 12 ft long
Weight 1760 lb to 1.5 tons
Life span 35 to 50 years
Predators Wild cats

Diet Black rhinos are herbivores and are browsers, not grazers. In the wild, they eat bushes and shrubs, preferring acacia, twigs and new growth.

Fact Black rhinos have really poor eyesight. This makes them unpredictable and dangerous, as they often charge at unfamiliar sounds and smells.

Conservation status — Critically endangered

- Mammals
- Placental mammals
- Hoofed mammals

Indian Rhinoceros
Rhinoceros unicornis

Factfile

Habitat	Tropical bushland, grassland, savannah
Distribution	Himalayas
Size	10 to 12.5 ft long
Weight	1.6 to 2.2 tons
Life span	45 to 50 years
Predators	Wild cats

Diet The Indian rhinoceros is a grazer that eats a large quantity of tall grass. It will also eat fruit, leaves and sometimes farm crops and some aquatic plants.

Fact The large horns of the rhinoceros are made from a protein called keratin. This is the substance that our fingernails and hair are made of.

Conservation status: Endangered

Malayan Tapir
Tapirus indicus

Mammals
Placental mammals
Hoofed mammals

Factfile

Habitat	Rain forest, jungle, rubber plantations
Distribution	Southeast Asia
Size	6 to 8 ft long
Weight	550 to 1200 lb
Life span	25 to 30 years
Predators	Tigers, leopards

Diet The Malayan tapir eats leaves, fruit and other plants, which it tugs with its nostrils that act like fingers. It will also graze on some underwater plants.

Fact The tapir's nose and upper lip combine into a flexible snout like an elephant's trunk. It can be used as a snorkel when the animal is under water!

Conservation status: Endangered

Mammals
Placental mammals
Hoofed mammals

South American Tapir
Tapirus terrestris

Factfile

Habitat	Tropical forest, swamp, lowland forests
Distribution	South America, predominantly in Brazil
Size	6.5 to 7 ft long
Weight	330 to 550 lb
Life span	Up to 30 years
Predators	Humans, jaguars

Diet This South American tapir feeds on leaves, buds, shoots, and small branches it tears from trees. It also eats some fruit, grasses and aquatic plants.

Fact The South American tapir differs from other tapirs due to its stiff mane or crest from shoulder to forehead. It grows to the size of a small pony.

Conservation status — **Vulnerable**

95

Wild Boar
Sus scrofa

Mammals

Placental mammals

Hoofed mammals

Factfile

Habitat Forest, shrubland
Distribution Europe, Asia, Africa, the Malay Archipelago
Size 5 to 7 ft long
Weight 110 to 772 lb
Life span Up to 20 years
Predators Humans, bears, crocodiles, snakes, large cats

Diet Wild boars eat a diet of fungi, vegetation, bulbs, grains, nuts, fruit, eggs, small vertebrates, invertebrates, carrion and even some manure!

Fact Humans are the main predators of wild boars. They may occasionally fall prey to very large predators, such as bears, large cats and crocodiles.

Conservation status **Least concern**

Mammals
Placental mammals
Hoofed mammals

Collared Peccary
Pecari tajacu

Factfile

Habitat Rain forest, desert
Distribution The Americas
Size 46 to 60 in long
Weight 33 to 55 lb
Life span 7 to 8 years
Predators Coyotes, pumas, jaguars

Diet Collared peccaries are mostly herbivorous. They eat roots, bulbs, fungi, nuts and fruits, as well as eggs, snakes, fish, frogs and occasional carrion.

Fact These animals have poor eyesight, but very good hearing and sense of smell. They are great runners, reaching speeds of up to 22 miles per hour.

Conservation status — Least concern

Common Warthog
Phacochoerus africanus

Mammals
Placental mammals
Hoofed mammals

Factfile

Habitat	Wooded savannah, steppe, semidesert
Distribution	Africa
Size	3 to 5 ft long
Weight	110 to 330 lb
Life span	15 to 18 years
Predators	Lions, leopards, cheetahs

Diet Common warthogs are grazers, who feast on large quantities of leaves, roots and tubers, wood, bark or stems, seeds, grains, nuts and fruit.

Fact Warthogs live in family groups called soundings. The group consists of females and their young. Males leave at 2 years of age and become solitary.

Conservation status — Least concern

- Mammals
- Placental mammals
- Hoofed mammals

Hippopotamus
Hippopotamus amphibius

Factfile

Habitat	Lakes, rivers, swamp
Distribution	Eastern, western and southern Africa
Size	10 to 16 ft long
Weight	1.4 to 4.8 tons
Life span	Up to 55 years
Predators	Lions, hyenas, crocodiles, humans

Diet Hippos graze on small shoots, grasses and reeds for between four and five hours each night. They usually consume around 88 pounds of food in this time.

Fact Hippos like to wallow in the mud during the day and sometimes doze in cool water for hours. They don't swim, but walk along on the riverbed.

Conservation status — Vulnerable

99

Bactrian Camel
Camelus bactrianus

Mammals
Placental mammals
Hoofed mammals

Factfile

Habitat	Arid regions, Siberian steppe, desert
Distribution	Asia
Size	Up to 7 ft tall
Weight	990 to 2200 lb
Life span	40 to 50 years
Predators	Gray wolves

Diet The Bactrian camel is able to eat even the driest, prickliest, and saltiest of plants. When plants are scarce they will eat bones, animals' skin or flesh.

Fact During the winter months the Bactrian camel will grow a thick, brown coat. They shed this shaggy coat when spring arrives and it gets warmer.

Conservation status: Endangered

Mammals
Placental mammals
Hoofed mammals

Dromedary Camel
Camelus dromedarius

Factfile

Habitat	Desert
Distribution	Middle East, India, Africa, Australia
Size	6 to 6.5 ft tall
Weight	880 to 1450 lb
Life span	Up to 40 years
Predators	No natural predators

Diet The dromedary camel eats primarily thorny plants, dry grasses and saltbush; however, they will eat most anything that grows in the desert.

Fact The camel's hump stores fat, which can be broken down into water when other sustenance is not available. They can travel up to 100 miles without water.

Conservation status — Not evaluated

Llama
Lama glama

| Mammals |
| Placental mammals |
| Hoofed mammals |

Factfile

Habitat	Mountainous desert, grasslands
Distribution	South America
Size	3 to 5 ft long
Weight	285 to 350 lb
Life span	15 to 20 years
Predators	Humans, pumas, coyotes

Diet The llama enjoys a diet of grass, leaves and young shoots. Unlike its relative the camel, the llama must drink often so prefers to be close to water.

Fact When llamas are angry they will stick their tongues out to express their dislike. They sometimes spit green, partially digested food too!

Conservation status: Least concern

Mammals
Placental mammals
Hoofed mammals

Guanaco
Lama guanicoe

Factfile

Habitat	Grassland, shrubland, occasional forest
Distribution	South America
Size	3.5 to 4 ft tall
Weight	Up to 300 lb
Life span	Up to 28 years
Predators	Pumas

Diet Guanacos are versatile foragers, browsing and grazing on grasses and plants. Like camels, they can go for long periods without water.

Fact When a female gives birth, her newborn, known as a chulengo, is able to walk immediately. Chulengos can keep up with the herd from birth.

Conservation status: Least concern

Red Deer
Cervus elaphus

Mammals
Placental mammals
Hoofed mammals

Factfile

Habitat	Woodland, swamp, forest
Distribution	Europe, Africa, Asia, N. America, Australasia
Size	5 to 9 ft long
Weight	377 to 1000 lb
Life span	Up to 25 years
Predators	Bears, coyotes, wolves, pumas, bobcats

Diet Red deer are browsers who enjoy feeding on grasses, sedges and forbs in summer, and woody growth in the winter months.

Fact Male red deer lose their antlers each March, but they begin to grow them back in May in preparation for the late-summer breeding season.

Conservation status — **Least concern**

Mammals
Placental mammals
Hoofed mammals

Fallow Deer
Dama dama

Factfile

Habitat	Forest, grassland, mountains, savannah
Distribution	Europe, Asia, the Americas, Africa, Australia
Size	4 to 6 ft long
Weight	75 to 175 lb
Life span	Up to 25 years
Predators	Wolves, cougars, bears, humans

Diet Fallow deer forage for vegetation, usually grasses, seeds and fruit. They will also eat herbs, dwarf shrubs, leaves, buds, shoots and bark.

Fact Females roam in groups with the young and the males roam in separate groups. The groups mix freely but only get close at breeding season.

Conservation status: Least concern

Reindeer
Rangifer tarandus

Mammals

Placental mammals

Hoofed mammals

Factfile

Habitat	Arctic tundra, subarctic forest
Distribution	Northern Europe, Alaska, Canada
Size	5 to 7.5 ft long
Weight	150 to 700 lb
Life span	10 to 15 years
Predators	Bears, wolves

Diet During the summer reindeers eat leaves, mushrooms, cotton grass and other vegetation. Lichens are an important part of their diet in winter.

Fact Reindeer antlers can measure 20 to 50 inches long on males, and 9 to 20 inches on females. Unlike horns, antlers fall off and grow back larger each year.

Conservation status — **Least concern**

Mammals
Placental mammals
Hoofed mammals

Moose
Alces alces

Factfile

Habitat Forest areas close to the Arctic tundra
Distribution North America and Europe
Size 6 to 7 ft tall
Weight 595 to 1590 lb
Life span 10 to 16 years
Predators Bears, wolves, humans

Diet Moose are so tall that they always prefer to browse higher grasses and shrubs because lowering their heads to ground level can be difficult.

Fact Moose do not have upper incisors or canine teeth and so they must nip off plants between a bony upper palate and their lower incisors.

Conservation status — **Least concern**

Giraffe
Giraffa camelopardalis

Mammals
Placental mammals
Hoofed mammals

Factfile

Habitat	Open woodland, savannah
Distribution	Sub-Saharan Africa
Size	14 to 20 ft tall
Weight	1700 to 2800 lb
Life span	Up to 25 years
Predators	Lions, leopards, hyenas

Diet Giraffes are known to eat up to 60 different species of plant throughout the year and do so by grabbing onto branches with their long, black tongues.

Fact Due to the giraffe's height and sensitive eyes, they are able to see for great distances. They have the greatest range of vision of any land animal.

Conservation status — **Least concern**

Mammals
Placental mammals
Hoofed mammals

Bongo
Tragelaphus eurycerus

Factfile

Habitat	Dense forest, bamboo thickets
Distribution	Western, Eastern and Central Africa
Size	5.5 to 8 ft long
Weight	460 to 890 lb
Life span	10 to 18 years
Predators	Pythons, leopards, hyenas, lions

Diet Bongos feed on leaves, roots, bark and grasses. They eat at night to keep them safer from the predators that they share their habitats with.

Fact To help them to cool down in the heat, bongos wallow in mud, which they then rub onto a tree as a way of polishing their smooth and heavy horns.

Conservation status — **Near threatened**

Greater Kudu
Tragelaphus strepsiceros

Mammals
Placental mammals
Hoofed mammals

Factfile

Habitat	Shrub woodland, savannah plains
Distribution	Eastern and southern Africa
Size	6 to 8 ft long
Weight	265 to 690 lb
Life span	8 to 14 years
Predators	Lions, leopards, wild dogs

Diet Kudus forage in woodland and thickets of shrubs for leaves from trees and bushes. Kudus also eat herbs, flowers, berries and fallen fruits.

Fact Baby kudus are born around February and March when the grass is at its highest and there is plenty of food to help the baby kudu to grow.

Conservation status: Least concern

Mammals
Placental mammals
Hoofed mammals

African Buffalo
Syncerus caffer

Factfile

Habitat	Open savannah, woodland, rain forest
Distribution	Sub-Saharan Africa
Size	6.5 to 11 ft long
Weight	661 to 2100 lb
Life span	18 to 25 years
Predators	Humans, lions

Diet African buffalo are herbivorous grazers. They graze on fresh grass, only turning to herbs, shrubs and some trees when fresh grass is scarce.

Fact African buffalo are capable swimmers. They have often been seen crossing deep rivers and lakes in order to find better grass for grazing.

Conservation status — Least concern

Yak
Bos grunniens

	Mammals
	Placental mammals
	Hoofed mammals

Factfile

Habitat	Alpine meadows, open hills
Distribution	Central Asia
Size	Up to 10.5 ft long
Weight	61 to 2200 lb
Life span	15 to 20 years
Predators	Humans, bears, wolves

Diet The yak is a herbivore and spends a great deal of time on grassy plains in the mountains, grazing on grasses, herbs, shrubs and wild flowers.

Fact During cold winter months the yak uses its dense horns to break through snow in order to reach the plants that are buried underneath.

Conservation status: Endangered

Mammals

Placental mammals

Hoofed mammals

American Bison
Bison bison

Factfile

Habitat	Grass plains, forest
Distribution	North America
Size	7 to 11.5 ft long
Weight	900 to 2200 lb
Life span	15 to 20 years
Predators	Wolves, bears, cougars, humans

Diet American bison graze on plains grasses, herbs, shrubs and twigs. They regurgitate their food and chew it as cud before final digestion.

Fact All bison wallow several times a day. They stir up dirt and roll around in the dust. The dusty cloud deters insects and may keep their bodies cool.

Conservation status — **Near threatened**

Gaur
Bos gaurus

Mammals
Placental mammals
Hoofed mammals

Factfile

Habitat	Evergreen, deciduous and savannah forest
Distribution	Southern Asia
Size	8 to 11 ft long
Weight	1500 to 2200 lb
Life span	18 to 25 years
Predators	Tigers, humans

Diet Gaurs are herbivores. They are browsers and grazers. They prefer green grass, but will consume dry grasses, flowering plants and leaves.

Fact When confronted by a tiger, the adult members of a herd form a circle surrounding the vulnerable young and calves, shielding them from danger.

Conservation status: Vulnerable

Mammals
Placental mammals
Hoofed mammals

Roan Antelope
Hippotragus equinus

Factfile

Habitat	Open or lightly wooded grassland
Distribution	Africa
Size	6 to 8 ft long
Weight	485 to 662 lb
Life span	15 to 17 years
Predators	Lions, leopards, hyenas, African hunting dogs

Diet Roan antelopes feed on grasses and other foliage in the morning and evening hours. They retreat to wooded areas during the middle of the day.

Fact Roan antelopes are brave and will confront predators, such as lions, using their horns as weapons. Many big cats have died during these fights.

Conservation status — **Least concern**

Black Wildebeest
Connochaetes gnou

Mammals
Placental mammals
Hoofed mammals

Factfile

Habitat	Grass plains, bush-covered savannah
Distribution	Africa
Size	4 to 5 ft tall
Weight	330 to 551 lb
Life span	15 to 20 years
Predators	Lions, cheetahs, crocodiles

Diet Wildebeest are grazers who prefer to eat short grass. They sense and follow rainstorms, trekking around 30 miles each day to find the best grass.

Fact Black wildebeest grow to around 5 feet tall but are relatively defenseless when faced with carnivorous predators such as lions and crocodiles.

Conservation status: Endangered

116

Mammals
Placental mammals
Hoofed mammals

Blue Wildebeest
Connochaetes taurinus

Factfile

Habitat	Bushland, woodland floodplains, savannah
Distribution	Eastern and southern Africa
Size	4 to 4.5 ft long
Weight	260 to 595 lb
Life span	Up to 20 years
Predators	Lions, cheetahs, spotted hyenas, wild dogs

Diet Blue wildebeest graze on grasses found on the savannah and the plains. When grasses are sparse, they may eat leaves from shrubs and trees.

Fact They are found in herds of about 20 to 30 animals, although some enormous herds have been recorded as having over a thousand members.

Conservation status: Least concern

Rocky Mountain Goat
Oreamnos americanus

Mammals
Placental mammals
Hoofed mammals

Factfile

Habitat	High-altitude mountains
Distribution	North America
Size	4 to 6 ft long
Weight	100 to 309 lb
Life span	12 to 15 years
Predators	Bears, coyotes, wolves

Diet The diet of the mountain goat includes grass, woody plants and moss. They get most of the water they need for survival from their food.

Fact They have powerful hind legs and can jump great distances. Their hooves have a slit in the middle to make them flexible on uneven ground.

Conservation status — Least concern

Mammals
Placental mammals
Hoofed mammals

Alpine Ibex
Capra ibex

Factfile

Habitat	Rocky cliffs, rolling slopes, bush
Distribution	Central Europe, Africa and Asia
Size	4 to 4.5 ft long
Weight	143 to 220 lb
Life span	10 to 18 years
Predators	Golden eagles, bears, wolves, leopards

Diet Ibexes tend to feed throughout the night in the forest, eating grasses, forbs, leaves, shoots and bark. They return to the rock cliffs in the morning.

Fact The horns continue to grow throughout their lifetime. An individual's age can be told from the annual rings visible on the back of the horns.

Conservation status — **Least concern**

Markhor
Capra falconeri

| Mammals |
| Placental mammals |
| Hoofed mammals |

Factfile

Habitat	Sparsely wooded cliff sides
Distribution	Western and central Asia
Size	4.5 to 6 ft long
Weight	70 to 240 lb
Life span	10 to 13 years
Predators	Wolves, snow leopards, lynx

Diet The markhor is a herbivorous animal that primarily grazes on a variety of vegetation including grasses, leaves, herbs, fruits and flowers.

Fact The markhor is a species of wild goat, easily identified by its long, white winter hair and the enormous spiraled horns that grow on the males.

Conservation status: Endangered

- Mammals
- Placental mammals
- Hoofed mammals

Bighorn Sheep
Ovis canadensis

Factfile

Habitat	Meadows, mountain slopes and foothills
Distribution	North America
Size	5 to 6 ft long
Weight	117 to 280 lb
Life span	6 to 15 years
Predators	Bears, coyotes, wolves

Diet During the summer, bighorn sheep feed on grasses or sedges. During the winter they eat more woody plants, such as willow and sage.

Fact Males have butting contests where they charge at each other at speed and crash their foreheads together. The fights can last for over 24 hours!

Conservation status: Endangered

Minke Whale
Balaenoptera bonaerensis

Mammals
Placental mammals
Ocean-living mammals

Factfile

Habitat	Oceans in temperate water
Distribution	Indian, Atlantic, Pacific Oceans, Antarctica
Size	22.5 to 33 ft long
Weight	up to 10 tons
Life span	30 to 50 years
Predators	Humans, sharks, orcas

Diet Minke whales feed on various crustaceans, plankton, and small schooling fish such as dogfish, anchovies, cod, eels, herring, mackerel and salmon.

Fact Minkes are fast swimmers who can reach speeds of 18 miles per hour. They are highly acrobatic and able to leap out of the water like dolphin.

Conservation status — **Near threatened**

- Mammals
- Placental mammals
- Ocean-living mammals

Orca
Orcinus orca

Factfile

Habitat	Ocean, coastal water
Distribution	Worldwide
Size	16.5 to 26 ft long
Weight	7.5 to 9.5 tons
Life span	50 to 60 years
Predators	Humans, large sharks

Diet Orcas feed on fish, squid, birds, and some marine mammals such as seals. Orca groups (called pods) often work together to catch a meal.

Fact Orcas (sometimes called killer whales) have been seen in every ocean around the world, but are most common in the Arctic and Antarctic oceans.

Conservation status **Endangered**

Bottlenose Dolphin
Tursiops truncatus

Mammals
Placental mammals
Ocean-living mammals

Factfile

Habitat   Temperate and tropical water
Distribution Worldwide
Size   8 to 13 ft long
Weight   500 to 1000 lb
Life span   20 to 35 years
Predators   Humans, sharks, orcas

Diet Dolphins eat most kinds of fish. Their diet also includes squid and small crustaceans such as shrimps. They swallow their food whole.

Fact Bottlenose dolphins will often approach boats and people in the water. They seem to enjoy human interaction and can be touched and petted.

Conservation status — Least concern

Mammals
Placental mammals
Sirenians

Dugong
Dugong dugon

Factfile

Habitat Warmer tropical waters, sea grass forest
Distribution Coastal waters of Africa, Asia, Australasia
Size 8 to 10 ft long
Weight 500 to 1000 lb
Life span 50 to 70 years
Predators Sharks, crocodiles

Diet Dugongs are sometimes called "sea cows" because they graze on sea grasses. These marine plants look like grass growing on a sandy sea floor.

Fact Dugongs can stay underwater for 6 minutes. They are sometimes seen balancing on their tails with their heads out of the water to breathe.

Conservation status Near threatened

Glossary

Arthropods Invertebrates with segmented bodies, external skeletons and jointed limbs. Examples include insects, spiders and crustaceans.

Browser An animal who feeds on leaves, young shoots and other vegetation.

Camouflage Colors or patterns that allow an animal to blend in with its background.

Canines (teeth) Sharp-pointed teeth on either side of the upper and lower jaw, meant for grasping and tearing food.

Carnivorous To feed on the flesh of other animals.

Carrion The remains of dead animals.

Colony A group of animals of the same type living together.

Crustaceans Arthropods such as lobsters or crabs with jointed legs and two pairs of antennae.

Cud Food brought up into the mouth by an animal from its stomach to be chewed again.

Dioecious trees Trees that are classed as either male or female.

DNA DNA is short for deoxyribonucleic acid. It is the material that carries all the information about how a living thing will look and function and is found in cells.

Folivorous An animal that chiefly eats leaves to survive.

Forb A broad-leaved herb other than a grass.

Grazer An animal that feeds on growing grasses and herbage.

Habitat The natural home of a species.

Haying The activity of cutting and drying grass to make hay.

Herbivore An animal that feeds on plants.

Hibernation To spend the winter in a sleeplike state.

Incisors The teeth at the very front of the mouth. They are the sharpest teeth, shaped to cut food and shovel it inward.

Invertebrates A group of animals without backbones.

Mineral lick A natural mineral deposit where animals in nutrient-poor ecosystems can obtain essential mineral nutrients.

Mustelids Mammals of the weasel family.

Nocturnal Active at night.

Omnivore An animal that feeds on plant and animal matter.

Pith The soft, spongelike, central cylinder of the stems of most flowering plants.

Plankton The tiny plant and animal organisms that float or drift in great numbers in fresh or salt water.

Predators Animals that kill and eat other animals.

Prey Animals hunted by predators.

Primates A group of mammals that includes some of the most intelligent animals, including humans, apes, monkeys, tarsiers, lemurs and lorises.

Regurgitate The act of bringing food that has been swallowed back to and out of the mouth.

Savannah Hot grassland in Africa.

Scavenger An animal that feeds on refuse and other decaying organic matter.

Steppe A dry, grassy plain. Steppes occur in temperate climates, which lie between the Tropics and polar regions.

Toxins Poisonous substances.

Tundra A treeless plain, especially of arctic regions, having a permanently frozen layer below the surface soil and plant life made up mostly of mosses, lichens, herbs and very small shrubs.

Ungulates Hoofed, herbivorous, four-legged animals such as horses, cattle, deer, pigs and elephants.

Vertebrate An animal with a backbone or spinal column. Examples include fish, amphibians, reptiles, birds and mammals.

Viviparous Producing living young instead of eggs from within the body in the manner of nearly all mammals, many reptiles and a few fish.

Index

Aardvark **16**
African buffalo **111**
African bush elephant **18**
African forest elephant **19**
African wild dog **56**
Alpine ibex **119**
Alpine marmot **30**
American bison **113**
American black bear **58**
American pika **27**
Arctic fox **48**
Arctic wolf **53**
Asiatic black bear **59**
Asiatic elephant **20**
Bactrian camel **100**
Bighorn sheep **121**
Black flying fox **46**
Black rhinoceros **92**
Black spider monkey **38**
Black wildebeest **116**
Blue wildebeest **117**
Bobcat **78**
Bongo **109**
Bornean orangutan **45**
Bottlenose dolphin **124**
Brown bear **60**
Brown-throated sloth **22**
Burchell's zebra **90**
California sea lion **62**
Capybara **29**
Caracal **79**
Cheetah **85**
Clouded leopard **83**
Collared peccary **97**
Common chimpanzee **43**
Common warthog **98**
Common wombat **10**
Coyote **55**
Dingo **54**
Dromedary camel **101**
Duck-billed platypus **8**
Dugong **125**
Eastern cottontail **26**
Eastern gray squirrel **31**
Emperor tamarin **39**
Eurasian badger **72**
Eurasian beaver **28**
Eurasian red squirrel **32**
Eurasian water shrew **14**
European hare **24**
European hedgehog **47**
European mole **15**
European rabbit **25**
Fallow deer **105**
Fennec fox **50**
Fishing cat **76**
Gaur **114**
Giant panda **61**
Giant pangolin **23**
Giraffe **108**
Golden lion tamarin **40**
Greater kudu **110**
Greater slow loris **33**
Grevy's zebra **91**
Gray seal **64**
Guanaco **103**
Hippopotamus **99**
Honey badger **73**
Iberian lynx **77**
Indian rhinoceros **93**
Indri **36**
Koala **9**
Leopard **84**
Leopard seal **65**
Lion **86**
Llama **102**
Lowland streaked tenrec **12**
Malayan tapir **94**
Maned wolf **52**
Markhor **120**
Meerkat **68**
Minke whale **122**
Moose **107**
Nine-banded armadillo **21**
Northern raccoon **66**
Northern river otter **75**
Ocelot **80**
Olive baboon **41**
Orca **123**
Polar bear **57**
Proboscis monkey **42**
Przewalski's wild horse **89**
Puma **82**
Raccoon dog **51**
Red deer **104**
Red fox **49**
Red howler monkey **37**
Red kangaroo **11**
Red panda **67**
Reindeer **106**
Ring-tailed lemur **34**
Roan antelope **115**
Rock hyrax **17**
Rocky mountain goat **118**
Sea otter **74**
Short-eared elephant shrew **13**
South American tapir **95**
Spotted hyena **88**
Stoat **70**
Striped hyena **87**
Striped skunk **69**
Tiger **81**
Verreaux's sifaka **35**
Walrus **63**
Western lowland gorilla **44**
Wild boar **96**
Wolverine **71**
Yak **112**